DRIVING DYNAMICS

BECOMING A BETTER, SAFER,
MORE EDUCATED DRIVER.

ANDRE R. LEVESQUE

First Edition: September 2014
Printed in the United States of America
ISBN-13: 978-1500879662
ISBN-10: 1500879665

DEDICATION

To my wife and daughter,
my family and friends, you mean the world to me.

Thank you for your love, support, your understanding,
and patience through it all.

PREFACE

After a great deal of observation, education and practical application to the driving world, I found the desire to assist the average driver. I wanted to do this by identifying the average driver and accelerate their knowledge in an application format, allowing them to understand the background reasoning and science behind the vehicles they drive. Driving Dynamics is a driver's guide to understanding basic physics and how both the driver and vehicle are in unison with each other. When the unison becomes singular it creates chaos. It is a driver's guide to understanding the basic conscious and subconscious thought process that coincides with driving the vehicle safely.

Driving Dynamics is an understanding that driving a motor vehicle is more than that. To understand the inner workings of the human element and the vehicle dynamics and mechanics allows you to be a safer, more educated driver.

Drive safe. Drive smart.

- Andy Levesque

ANDRE R. LEVESQUE

TABLE OF CONTENTS

Chapter 5 (continued)

INTRODUCTION

Driving Dynamics is driver education that transforms current driver habits back to the basics of driving skills while enhancing the driver's perspective and connection between the driver and the vehicle. Driving Dynamics is all about the Driver and the Vehicle; not the Driver vs. the Vehicle. A proper and educated merger between the driver and vehicle creates safe driving skills while experiencing the full capability of the vehicle.

Those of us that drive vehicles need to understand that operating a vehicle, in and of itself, is the ultimate multitasking event. Operating or driving a vehicle encompasses a multitude of tasks that include thousands of thought processes per second; most of which we are unaware. To learn and comprehend this is a feat all in itself. To be conscious of all that does occur while driving, and all than can occur, transforms these skills from static to dynamic.

Most of us have attended some form of driver education program to obtain our driver's license. Some have gone to a driver education school, some have read the books, learned from parents, took a practical test and presto, you are licensed driver! Whichever way, we learned the very basic rules of the road, how to park, and basic (I sarcastically reiterate the word "basic") operations of the vehicle. A small percentage of drivers take the time to further educate themselves and obtain advanced driving skills and ability through specialized training. Very few driver education programs educate how a driver should observe, process data, and respond to the information received; then, how to apply that information and use a multitude of psychomotor skills to operate the vehicle correctly. Mere effort to understand that it can take all of this in a millisecond to occur, projects you and provides an open mind into driving dynamics.

This text will help you better understand the inner workings of how a driver and vehicle are an extension of one another, how a vehicle acts and responds, how a driver should act or react, and how it all comes together. Driving dynamics is defined as the operation of a motor vehicle combining the human element coupled with the mechanical and physical characteristic features that the vehicle can deliver together. In other words, combining the driver actions and reactions, coupled with the physical forces placed upon the vehicle and the mechanical limitations of the vehicle, is driving dynamics.

There is more to just sitting behind the wheel of a car, starting the car, putting it into gear and zooming away. If it was that simple, we would all be experts as drivers and collisions would never happen. Understanding how the physical use of force and motion affects the actions and responses of the vehicle. Now add in the human element of the equation and what do you get? A tangled mess of individual dynamic forces all competing to operate in unison.

The human brain utilizes multitask processes by using the visual input of the eyes, motor commands to the arms, hands, feet, all the subconscious operations of the brain, and all within an instant. The brain then utilizes stored learned memory to apply the correct technique in order to operate a machine; a machine that is ultimately controlled by the use of natural forces and physics.

Driving Dynamics will address these issues independently allowing a full understanding and a unison medley of human input, the physical limitations of the vehicle and the use of physical forces. Some physics will be discussed but it is at a simple level for all to understand.

Welcome to Driving Dynamics!

CHAPTER 1

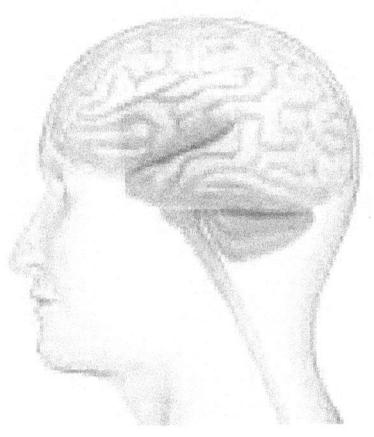

MIND GAMES

ANDRE R. LEVESQUE

Cognitive Thoughts and Decision Making

We, as human beings, as creatures of this Earth, as biological objects, have developed what is now labeled cognitive thought. While all creatures have an instinctual thought process, human beings have moved forward in development and began the cognitive thinking process. Cognitive is defined as, "of, relating to, being, or involving conscious intellectual activity (as thinking, reasoning, or remembering" (Mririam-Webster, 2014).

At lightning speeds, sometimes immeasurable, our subconscious thought process begins deciding if the problem at hand is a life or death situation. This decision of 'Fight or Flight' is instinctual in most organisms. With any imminent threat of death or physical harm, the subconscious mind instinctively reacts in a survival mode decision process, bypassing any immediate cognitive thought. This subconscious action is a life-saving system hard wired into our brain. For example, when we were children and placed our hand on the hot stove, our body immediately reacted away from the heat source to prevent injury. Our memory process stored the negative experience as bad or caution in the event of further encounters. With training and practice, one can learn to work in conjunction with the fight or flight system and even override or modify physical and mental responses.

With cognitive thought comes learned behavior. Creatures have instinctual behavior that has evolved over thousands or even millions of generations. Primitively, most creatures have what is called learned behavior. Simply, this means that behavior does not occur until it is learned. Most of what we have for knowledge is in fact, learned behavior. What human beings do not have is the ability to choose what race we are, who we are born to, where we are born, and what early stages of our environment in which we are raised. Humans learn from and are taught by parents, elders, family, friends, government, religion, media, etc. We are taught to like, dislike, hate, love, ridicule, and nurture. Moral values or deciding what is right or wrong is learned behavior.

When a child is first born, there are instinctual acts that occur. Experts report that for a brief amount of time, most acts of an infant are instinctual until the age of 6 months. After that, most behavior is learned through visual and audible stimulation. This progresses to language that is taught by the parents or caregivers. The time of adolescence is a learning sponge and is direction forming especially when the child reaches adolescence. The more exposure the child receives, the more opportunity there is to learn. Also in this phase is the beginning of the most basic concept we have, yes or no and good or bad.

Exposure brings potential for conflict. A child learns from experience or from teaching how to solve conflict. The child begins to learn the positives and the consequences of the decision. Although it is not recognized by the child, the conscious efforts are being recorded into their memory. For each positive and negative result, each is stored respectively. This process continues throughout our lives. It is how we respond to and react to the conflict that defines us as a person and collectively as a group.

We as people make decisions. We have choices; life or

death, good or bad, right or wrong, even a simple yes or no. What we do not realize is the in-depth, multi-step process one must endure during this decision process. We are always making decisions, many of which we do not even realize. For someone to say, "I am not making decisions today" is untrue. The mere fact that they are not making decisions today is in fact, a decision. We chose to wake up on time or sleep in. We chose to bathe ourselves at the start of the day or not. We decide if and when we are leaving the house for work or school. Most are not recognizable as a conscious thought but merely an option, a choice, a decision. Regardless of semantics one thing is for sure, we all make decisions.

Every decision you make will affect you or someone else. This is very important and should be understood. What some people are not able to determine is to what degree it will affect either you or someone else. It could be as simple as deciding how much salt I put on my food, or as complex as governmental policy making, for example. Grand decisions are more complex. Complex problems create the potential for a multitude of solutions that can affect one person, a few, or many in all ranges of good to bad. It can be as simple as changing someone's mood or change their life forever.

For example, your birthday is next month. Do you want a party? Have you been asked to have a party for others to celebrate? Are you celebrating for yourself or for others? When will you have the party? Where will you have the party? Who will pay for the party? How many will you invite? Who do you invite? Why them and not others? With a simple decision to celebrate your own birthday, hundreds or sometimes thousands of decisions and considerations must be made and it is continuous, even after the party. Some people go to extremes making decisions, others are basic. We are human. We make mistakes, we make our fortunes.

Direct or indirect decisions can cause problems. Even accidental or unintentional decisions made can really affect you or someone else. Some direct decisions are made but the indirect actions causes the problem. These are considered consequences. For example, the mere fact of texting on your mobile phone is a conscious decision not really affecting others, only to the recipient. However when that decision is made while driving a car, now the web of consequences opens and possibilities become endless. You could in fact successfully text and drive, but not likely. You may end up in a crash. If it is a fender bender, you are lucky. But what else have you set in motion because of your decision to text and drive? Let us take a look.

Because you chose to text and drive, you increased a likelihood of collision. This is considered risk or liability. When in actual physical control of a motor vehicle (driving a car) and you hit another vehicle, cause injury or death to someone else, or damage property, you are now liable. Most states require us to hold a minimum amount of auto liability insurance to protect us for such an event. In many cases the car crash is minor, no one injured and the cars go to the shop and get fixed. So what is the big deal? Your decision affected yourself and someone else, now in a negative way. You will have to file a claim on your insurance. Your insurance company will decide how much of the damage is out-of-pocket for you and how much they will pay. The other person will have to do the same with their insurance company. Now, one or both parties need a vehicle. Who will pay? Who will go without? Who will get a new vehicle and who will have to settle? How much of each drivers life and or family has been displaced? This ripple effect can be minor or major depending on the collision, not to mention all the decisions you will have to make and how it will affect you or someone else.

On the flip side, consider the decisions that the insurance company will make and how that affects you. Don't forget legal issues as well. You can get a traffic citation if you are in violation and depending on the violation it may be a criminal matter. You may get sued from the other party. You may have both a criminal and civil matter going at the same time. If it is a criminal matter such as manslaughter (causing the death of another), jail and fines are in your future. How will you pay the fines? Will you lose your job while you are in jail and now have a criminal record? What about a mandatory license suspension? Can you afford the inconvenience of not having your license and having someone else drive you around? Don't forget about the attorney fees. That is in the thousands of dollars!

This process continues well beyond the collision. It even affects you insurance rates, based on risk factors. Remember liability? WOW! It never seems to end. This is all because you wanted to send a friend text or chose to drink and drive. You probably did not realize you had to think of all of this before sending that text while driving. You did not think it all the way through, did you? True, you did not have to think of it all, but it can all happen when you do not think ahead and consider consequences.

In the world of physics, Sir Isaac Newton revealed that for every action there is an equal and opposite reaction. This can be applied to most anything; force, relationships, communication, etc. For humor's sake, most men would agree that for every male action there is an equal and opposite female reaction, or vice versa!

Many choices are simple and harmless. But those once in a while decisions that have to be made can be a doozy. For some it is an eye opener and a lesson learned, for some it is catastrophic. Generally, we are not aware of the full extent of our actions and how it may affect us until it has gone to an extreme or beyond our norm. By then, it may be too late. Take the time to think ahead. Ask someone that is knowledgeable or trustworthy the questions that need an answer.

Remember, *"Every decision you make will affect you and or someone else!"*

- Andre Levesque

CHAPTER 2

Sir Isaac Newton (1642–1727)

THE LAWS OF MOTION

ANDRE R. LEVESQUE

I will openly admit that this section of the text may seem a bit dry, but it is important to understand the principals of physics and how it relates to driving a vehicle. Physics is in every aspect of driving as it relates to the vehicle and vehicle response to the driivng input. I have tried to write this section for all to understand and provide examples as it relates to everyday driving. Let us take a look at the forces of nature.

<u>Forces of Nature</u>

A motor vehicle is a machine. Machines are designed to produce. Machines operate under the principals of mechanical and motion forces. Motor vehicles operate under basic and advanced principals of different forms of physics. A few hundred years ago, Sir Isaac Newton worked on developing calculus and physics at the same time. During his work, he came up with the three basic ideas that are applied to the physics of most motion. These theories have been tested and verified so many times over the years, that scientists now call them Newton's Three Laws of Motion. This portion is a very basic physics lesson to understand how a vehicle operates in regards to the laws of physics and motion.

Vehicles operate in a wide array of physical forces including but not limited to; gravitational force (the force that pulls us to the Earth), frictional force (the force that keeps the vehicle from sliding all over the roadway), air resistance force (the force against the vehicle as it progresses forward or reverse), the applied forces of torque (the twisting of the vehicle or turning of the wheels), motion (directional, lateral, and rotational), and velocity (speed), just to name a few. We have all experienced these forces in one form or another in life and not necessarily in a vehicle. The vehicle, in and of itself and in all its glory, is a mechanical marvel designed to progress the machine in a direction of our choosing whether it be forward, reverse, and to steer the machine in a variety of directions; all while incorporating and operating within the limitations of these applied forces.

Newton's First Law

One of the laws and principals developed was Newton's first law: "Every object persists in its state of rest or uniform motion in a straight line unless it is compelled to change that state by forces impressed on it" (NASA, National Aeronautics and Space Administration, 2014) (see *Figure 1*). Simply, an object does not move unless a different force moves it. This is further investigated and expanded upon by astronomer Galileo and is often referred to "The Law of Inertia." Inertia is a force best described in the following example.

You are driving your vehicle and have to make a sudden stop. You feel yourself being pushed into the seatbelt but all other loose objects in the vehicle now move forward and on to the floorboard. This is Inertia. First, you were traveling at a steady rate of speed and then forced to stop. The seatbelt prevented you from moving forward, and in fact, reacted against Inertia. *Figures 2* and *Figure 3* depict the same action but as a passenger standing on a train, bus or other motion vehicle (TutorVista, 2014). Both the vehicle and the person are at a constant rate of speed until it changes or slows.

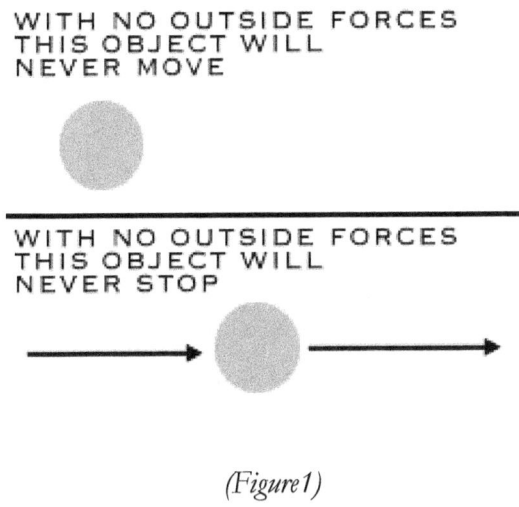

(Figure1)

When enacted by a change in velocity or braking by the vehicle, the objects in the vehicle are not slowing as fast as the vehicle and therefore have the feeling they are being forced forward. In fact it is not the change of velocity or speed on the person but that of the vehicle and all contents within the vehicle. The seatbelt acts as a limiter or a reducer of the force. The same happens when a vehicle accelerates. You feel like you are being pushed backwards. Actually you and the vehicle were at a constant state of rest. The vehicle accelerated forward and forced you along with it giving the feeling you are being pushed backwards.

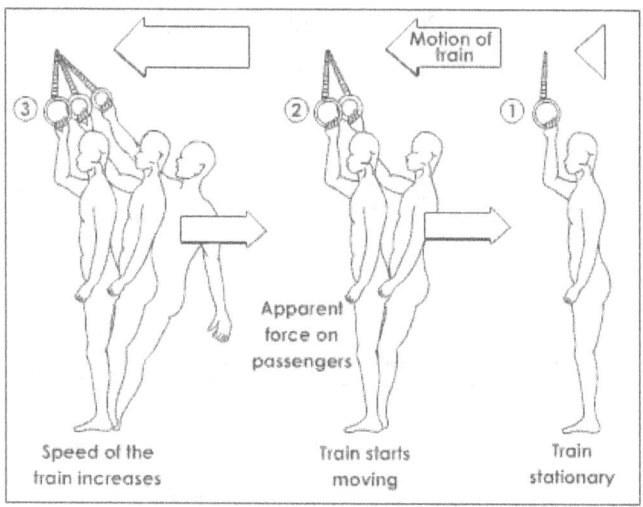

(Figure 2)

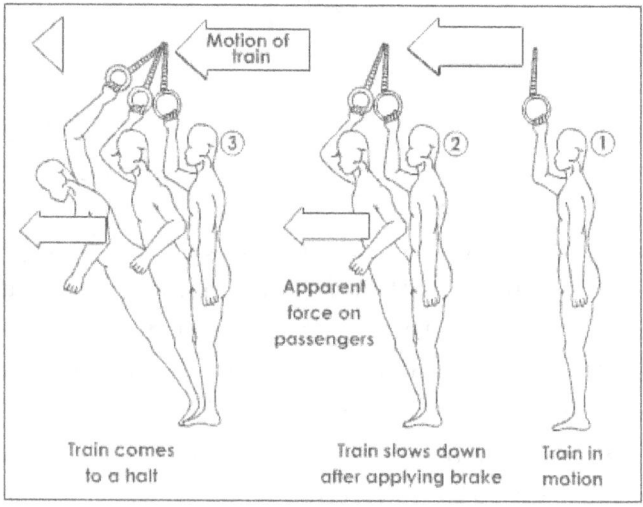

(Figure 3)

Newton's Second Law

Newton's second law seems more complicated but it actually defines "Force." The law informs us that objects at equilibrium (the condition in which all forces balance) will not accelerate. According to Newton, the law explains how the velocity (speed) of an object changes when it is subjected to an external force. An object will only accelerate if there is a net or unbalanced force acting upon it. The presence of an unbalanced force will accelerate an object, changing speed, direction, or both speed and direction. "Force is equal to the change in momentum (mV) per change in time. For constant mass, force equals mass times acceleration" (NASA, National Aeronautics and Space Administration, 2014). From this, Newton derived a formula that Force = mass multiplied by acceleration (F=ma). Mass is a measure of the inertia in a body or the amount of material in a body. It appears that mass and weight are the same. In fact, they are not. They are, however related. Actually, weight equals mass multiplied by the acceleration of gravity (W=mg). Since the acceleration of gravity is essentially the same on the surface of the earth (32.2 ft/sec^2) we can think of weight as a measurement of mass.

Newton's Second Law and developed formula F=ma is, in simple terms, described as the faster and harder you move something, the further it will travel. Simply, if you kick a ball softly it will not travel as far as if you kicked with all your might. Newton's second law seems more complicated but it actually defines "Force." The law informs us that objects at equilibrium (the condition in which all forces balance) will not accelerate. According to Newton, the law explains how the velocity (speed) of an object changes when it is subjected to an external force. An object will only accelerate if there is a net or unbalanced force acting upon it. The presence of an unbalanced force will accelerate an object, changing speed, direction, or both speed and direction. "Force is equal to the change in momentum (mV) per change in time. For constant mass, force equals mass times acceleration" (NASA, National Aeronautics and Space Administration, 2014). From this, Newton derived a formula that Force = mass multiplied by acceleration (F=ma). Mass is a measure of the inertia in a body or the amount of material in a body. It appears that mass and weight are the same. In fact, they are not. They are, however related. Actually weight = mass x acceleration of gravity. Since the acceleration of gravity is essentially the same on the surface of the earth ($32.2 \, ft/sec^2$) we can think of weight as a measurement of mass.

Newton's Second Law and formula F=ma is, in simple terms, described as the faster and harder you move something, the further it will travel. The best example would be if you kick a ball softly it will not travel as far as if you kicked with all your might.

Newton's Third Law

Newton's third law is very common with every day events. According to Newton, "Every object persists in its state of rest or uniform motion in a straight line unless it is compelled to change that state by forces impressed on it." This is also known as the famous version, "For every action, there is an equal and opposite re-action. (NASA, National Aeronautics and Space Administration, 2014)" *Figure 4* shows an easy example of this. If you blow up a balloon then release it, what happens? The balloon makes funny noises as the air escapes the valve. More so, all three of Newton's laws are in effect. The air is released by the pressure of the stretched balloon wall. The air is forced through the valve causing it to escape with pressure. The pressure of air escaping forces in one direction and the balloon reacts and travels in the opposite direction. It is a fun and realistic experiment. Even better, it is a simpler and more thorough explanation of the three laws all working together in unison and separately all at the same time. Try it out! You may get some giggles out of it too!

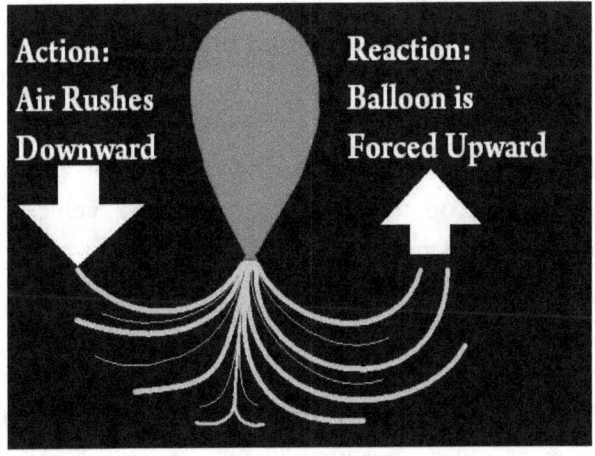

(Figure 4)

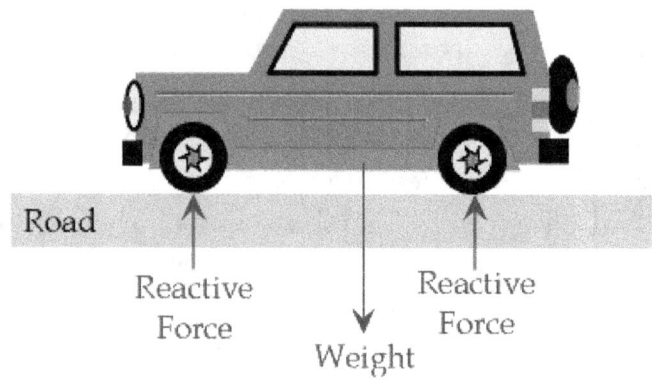

(*Figure 5*)

Figure 5 depicts Newton's laws as it relates to automobiles. The vehicle weight equals mass. The vehicle weight is countered by the reaction force of gravity pushing up against the vehicle. At rest, this force is equal. The vehicle is then accelerated forward by the wheels using rotational torque (force). The wheels are kept in check as an opposing force by the friction on the road surface. The driving force of the vehicle moving forward has an equal and opposite force or wind resistance as the vehicle moves forward. Is it making sense yet? I hope so.

Gravity

Let us weigh in on gravity. Gravity is a universal force that attracts objects proportionately according to mass or size. In other words, a smaller object will be attracted to a larger object. These proportions are at great numbers and complex. ALL objects attract each other with a force of gravitational attraction. Gravity will keep us standing on the surface of the Earth, just as our cars stay on the road. The mass of the Earth is far greater than the mass of a person or a vehicle, therefore attracting smaller objects inward or toward the center of the Earth. Gravity is part of Newton's Third Law. The Earth pulls the object toward the surface. When the force (mass of the object) comes in contact with the Earth, the Earth in turn, pushes back equally as seen in Figure 5. The force pushing back is actually the centripetal force of the rotating planet Earth (*Figure 5*).

Wow! You were not expecting all that. For all you were concerned, you start the car, put it in gear, press on the gas pedal and vroom, off you go. Little did you know this is just the beginning. All of these forces, plus others, are always present and active whether you want them or not. It is important to understand these basic laws of physics while you learn to operate the vehicle. We can only learn to drive within the laws of physics. Anytime you try to beat Newton's Laws of Physics, Newton's Laws are always present and will prevail.

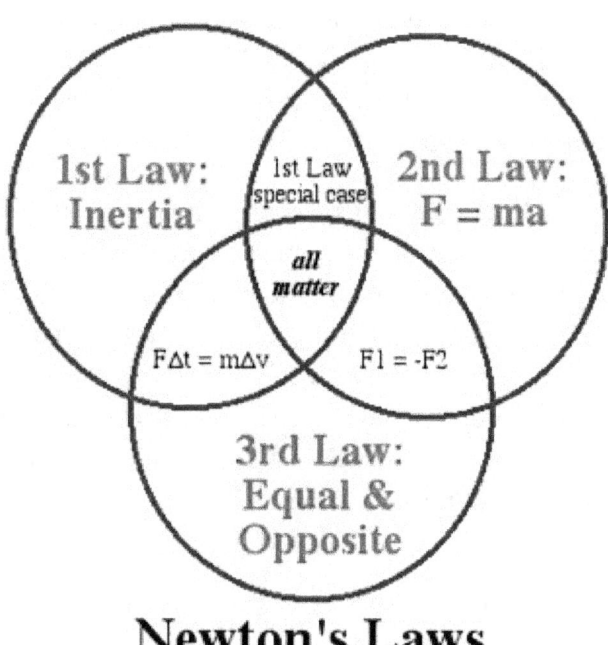

Newton's Laws

CHAPTER 3

THE DRIVER

ANDRE R. LEVESQUE

The Driver

Driving a motor vehicle is a level of responsibility that many are not aware or fail to recognize. Many drivers do not recognize the real dangers of operating a motor vehicle and fail to focus their attention to the operation of that vehicle. Driver distraction is a major human factor in vehicle collisions today and began when the motor vehicle was first developed. The first drivers were distracted with the multitasking of controlling the vehicle, passenger conversations, vehicle features, the weather and elements, external distractions, traffic, and more.

Not much has changed in the 100 plus years of driving motor vehicles. In fact, car manufacturers and engineers have designed a smoother operation of the machine, added more internal distractions through visually appealing interior gauges, dashboard configurations, audio and entertainment features, and more. In other words, more buttons, more luxury, more distractions!

It is easy for a person to get distracted, never mind while driving a motor vehicle and all the features contained within. *Figure 6* is a picture of a 1910 Oldsmobile. It does not appear to have all the bells and whistles that the 2015 BMW displays in *Figure 7*, but the basics are still present. Both vehicles have a motor which supplies power to a gear system, a steering mechanism, accelerator and braking system. In both vehicles, the driver must drive the vehicle without colliding into other objects. Yet in the 100 plus years of designing motor vehicles, only the vehicles designs have changed, not so much for the driver. Vehicles still collide into objects; not on their own accord, but at the hand of human control.

(Figure 6)

(Figure 7)

When driving, many are more concerned about issues that have nothing to do with driving the vehicle. Some talk on cell phones, talk to passengers, eating or drinking, finding a better radio station, some are texting, and so much more. The problem at hand is that the driver is not concentrating on the designated task which is, driving. Society today has transformed people so they are driven to distraction. Limit these distractions while driving and do one thing while in the driver seat of a motor vehicle. Drive the vehicle. Easier said than done, right? Right!

The secret skill is to limit distractions and focus on operating the vehicle. We have all been in that distracted situation and some sort of driving emergency occurs. The difference between a regular driver and a dynamic driver is anticipating potential problems in advance and learning how to respond to these problems as they appear in emergent situations.

Physical and emergent reaction is hard wired or a subconscious action in the mind that creates an instant decision of fight or flight. Naturally, we all want to avoid danger and injury. That is the flight portion of the reaction. How we respond to dangerous situations is behavior that is learned and should be rehearsed. By understanding these differences defines the dynamic driver, prepares the driver for unforeseen circumstances and emergency maneuvers to avoid a collision. Merely applying the brakes may not be enough or may not be the proper solution to avoid collision(s). The natural response to avoid injury is to travel away from the danger.

In *Figure 8* the danger path can be whatever danger you choose; an animal, a vehicle, a pedestrian, etc. The driver path is your travel route. As it depicts, a natural reaction for the driver is to brake and or move away from the approaching danger. In this example, it actually places the driver closer to danger and increases your potential for collision. This maneuver is normal and is a natural reaction. If a collision is inevitable, this type of angular collision reduces a head on collision and reduces potential for serious injury. In other words, the smaller the angle of collision (less than 90 degrees), the likelihood for serious injury is reduced.

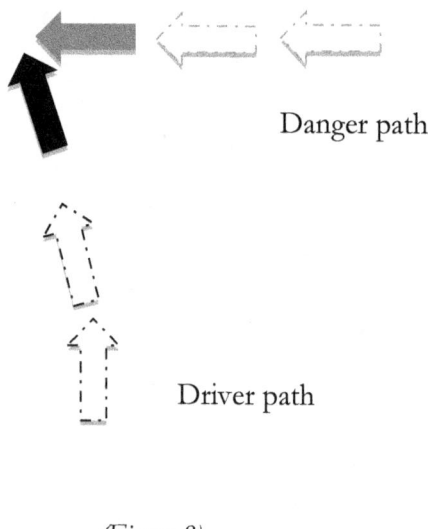

Danger path

Driver path

(Figure 8)

In some cases, as rare as they are, it may be necessary to drive towards the rear of the danger in order to limit the collision forces. The best example is avoiding the approaching danger. The danger is approaching in a straight or linear line across your path. The natural reaction for a driver is to avoid the collision and steer the vehicle in the direction the danger is traveling. In this case, emergency braking and steering will limit collision potential.

If the driver brakes and steers towards the rear of the approaching danger, chances are greater that the danger will continue to move away from your vehicle path. This places your vehicle in an area where the danger is no longer; therefore limiting the chance for collision. *Figure 9* below depicts this maneuver.

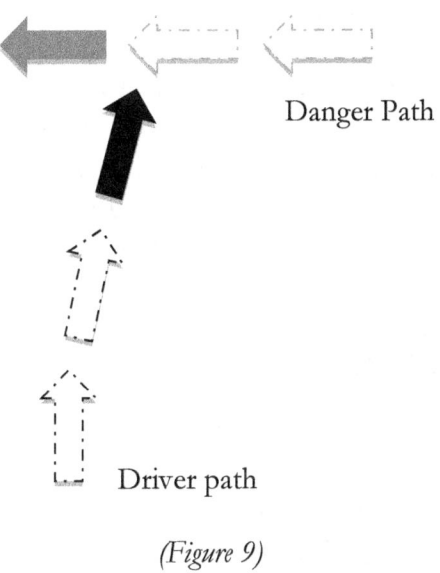

Danger Path

Driver path

(Figure 9)

On the other hand, it also increases the chance of driving into a secondary incident and emergency that the driver has to anticipate and react against. This is why utilizing the S.I.P.D.E. and Smith-System driving is important to practice all the time. These driving systems will be discussed later on in the book (Driving Systems, page 43).

A dynamic driver must always view the roadway well in advance of the vehicle and constantly scan approaching intersections for opposing traffic. Not one or two car lengths but way down the road. Don't forget to continue to view all around you by using the rear view mirrors. It is equally important to evaluate situations behind you (in the same direction) as it is in front of you. Collisions are not always to the front, many are to the rear and sides.

Important note – It is always best to avoid a true 'head on' collision at all costs. The forces at work in a linear 180 degree collision are too great. Any actions to create an angular collision will greatly increase survivability and reduce injury to the occupants.

Driver Attitude

We all have attitudes. They surround us all day; positive, negative, fake and genuine. But when it comes to driving, we see so many types of attitudes in so many different drivers. Let's face it, if we all had the same right attitude, we would have fewer crashes. Realistically, for each individual person, there is a different attitude and that changes all day long. At the least, we should all have a safe and defensive attitude when we drive.

Having a positive driving attitude includes being focused on driving the vehicle, always thinking ahead, limiting your internal and external distractions, getting out of the bad mood you were in and leave it behind you when you get in the driver's seat. Being angry is one of the worst attitudes to have when behind the wheel. It causes the driver to take out frustration while behind the wheel, causing erratic driving, unsafe speed, unsafe lane changes and other forms of road rage. Being a dynamic driver is having the ability to reduce the anger or stress and leaving it somewhere else when driving.

Your attitude will reflect on your driving. In other words, your attitude will broadcast through your driving. When I was a law enforcement officer specializing in traffic enforcement, I could read driver's attitudes by the way they were driving. Mostly during the daytime, if someone was swerving in their lane, they were most likely distracted either on the phone, having a conversation or utilizing some electronic device like a GPS or cell phone. At night it was possible, but some erratic drivers were impaired through drinking or drugs, some are just inattentive or have difficulty with their vision at night.

Younger driver attitudes are much different than the older or mature driver attitude. Some like to speed and show off their attitude, some like to speed to impress someone in their car, others just because they feel like it for no apparent reasons. That is not a safe attitude to have. That is dangerous and erratic driving that becomes a liability.

Driving attitude has much to do with being safety minded. Those that drive with patience and defensively are less likely to be at fault in a collision than those that are aggressive and impatient. When we see erratic driving, aggressive or even hostile drivers, stay clear! They will draw you into a very bad situation that may not end well. If someone is driving aggressively near you or is as a result of a driving mistake that caused an issue, the best advice is to correct yourself and continue on your way. The aggressive driver may not be involved in collisions, but may cause collisions around them due to their actions. Be aware.

Do not engage the aggressive driver. Let the aggressive driver go on their way by themselves. Do not react and fuel a fire that is already lit. Let their bad day continue to be their bad day and not yours. Be sure that your attitude does not affect your driving or someone else. In other words, be sure your behavior and driving attitude is where it should be, focused on driving the best you can.

Only drive within your skills and abilities. Over-driving a vehicle beyond your skills will lead to a bad result. Your driving attitude should never reach beyond your driving ability. When that does occur, you are over-driving the vehicle. Such behavior will lead to poor driving and even worse, potential for a crash. Drive within your ability and comfort level. If you are not comfortable driving at high speeds, heavy traffic or interstate driving, use alternative routes. There is always more than one way to get somewhere. If you know of only one way, learn more! Being honest with your self is the first step.

Drive within the rules of the road. Do not make up your own rules of the road; use the ones already in place. If someone is driving aggressively against you or even made a mistake that resulted in evasive actions on your part, breathe and let it go. If someone is adamant in merging in front of you, let them in. If they cut you off in traffic, slow down and give them room. Aggressive driving leads to high risk of collision. Being a courteous driver saves aggression and allows you to see the entire picture of the roadway. As your vision closes in on a target, the more likely you are to cause a problem. The wider your vision or field of focus, the less likely you are to be involved in a collision as you can observe more.

The Eyes Have It!

Of all our or senses; smell, taste, touch, sight and sound, sight is the most prominent sensory used while driving. From least important to most important would be taste, smell, sound, touch and sight. There is little to no reason why we need to use our taste to operate a vehicle. Smell may be important to recognize issues with the vehicle or outside of the vehicle. Becoming more important is sound. Sound alerts us to the surrounding environment outside the vehicle such as traffic or issues with the vehicle we are driving. Drowning out the environment sound with a great stereo will not benefit the driving situation. Touch is important to sense the steering wheel and foot pedals, but sight is most important.

The majority of what we do when we drive a vehicle is look with our eyes. We are consciously and constantly using our senses from the time we wake in the morning to the time we fall asleep at night. Even while we sleep we use our senses subconsciously. When we drive a car, sight is most important. We need to see where we want to go, where we are going and where we have been by using our mirrors.

When driving, vision is best used eyes wide open. In other words, utilize and learn to utilize all of your vision potential. There is more to vision than focusing straight ahead. The human eye can see about 180 degrees (some may see 190 degrees). Granted, our eyes are in the front of our head, but there is more in our line of vision than just straight ahead. People that train themselves to utilize their peripheral vision have a better sense of their surroundings than those that do not. Peripheral vision is what the mind can sense from the furthest left and furthest right without moving your head.

About one quarter of the human brain is involved in visual processing - more than any other sense. Arguably the most closely studied of the five main senses, the Society for Neuroscience claims that more is known about vision than any other vertebrate sensory system. In general, a pair of healthy human eyes has a total field of view of approximately 200 degrees horizontally (left and right), about 120 degrees of which are shared by both eyes, and 135 degrees vertically (up and down). These values tend to decrease with age and vision becomes limited.

Remember that the eye is a complex organ, mostly utilized as a camera for the brain. Cameras focus on what the user wants to gather for information. When it comes to the eye, widen the perspective and more information can be gathered. The potential for danger can be observed and recognized faster than when the eye is limited on a single object or task. When someone limits the focus of attention it is called tunnel vision.

As this applies to driving, regular driving should utilize the widest possible use of vision until an area of concern becomes visible. The mind will automatically communicate with the eyes to focus on the danger and report back to the brain. The brain then processes the data and responds to the attentive area in view. Sometimes it is danger, possible danger, an automatic eye attractant of a moving object, etc. Regardless, utilizing the widest possible view will most likely perceive danger faster or earlier than the other drivers. If a driver looks straight ahead all the time, they have a limited field of view and are more at risk for collisions either at their fault or not able to avoid collisions from the actions of the other driver(s). In the event of night driving, most drivers are limited to the headlamp light output. In this case, it is important to keep the headlamps clean and clear as well as the windshield clean to reduce glare and visibility. It also reduces eye fatigue, which will cause tunnel vision and reduced visibility.

Since the eyes are the most important sensory organ we have as it relates to driving, take care of them. Get regular eye exams, wear your glasses or contact lenses as prescribed, and use sunglasses with UVA, UVB and UVC protection as well as polarized lenses to reduce glare. It helps to keep the eyes healthy and reduces defects as we age. Speaking of clear vision, keep all glass clean and free from smear and smudges both inside and outside. Clean glass reduces glare on the eyes constant eye strain and limits the opportunity to miss important actions on the roadway.

Seatbelts

It should go without mention, but not everyone wears a seatbelt. Most states have now required the proper use of a seatbelt restraining device. The message is simple; it reduces injury potential and saves lives. I am already hearing the opposing side of the argument. "I know someone that was involved in a major car crash and lived because they were not wearing a seatbelt". Well they rolled the dice and got lucky. Seatbelts do not save *all* lives or prevents *all* injuries. It does, however, greatly reduce the risk of serious injury or death.

From what we have learned in other chapters, the forces of physics cannot be changed. As the saying goes, "It is not the fall that will kill you, it is the sudden stop that will kill you." That is correct. In the form of physics, it is the rapid change in velocity or momentum that will cause severe injury or death. The ΔV (Delta V or change in velocity (speed)) or the ΔP (Delta P or change in momentum) will mess up the body. It is the sudden change in direction with a great amount of force that the body cannot withstand, therefore causes severe injury or death.

Seatbelts do many things. It restricts the forward movement in the event of a frontal collision, it limits the lateral movement of the occupant in the event of a side collision and most importantly, it keeps the occupant or driver in their seat! The argument for not wearing the seatbelts is heard all over. "It is too tight", "I cannot breathe", "It is in my way", blah, blah, blah.

Seatbelt engineers have come a long way to make it more comfortable. Seatbelts now release and retract with ease of movement and they even adjust higher or lower to fit most statures. If the manufacturer seatbelt does not fit or buckle due to your physique, check with your vehicle manufacturer for a seatbelt extending device. There really is no excuse for not wearing a seatbelt. It does save lives, perhaps even your own.

I preach this from my own experience. Many moons ago as a driver with limited experience, I was driving to work on a back road in rural Maine. I was traveling downhill approaching an intersecting road. My road had no stop sign or traffic light. The intersecting road had a stop sign. I observed a vehicle stopped at the sign to my right. I continue down the hill and was quickly approaching the intersection. As I arrived at the intersection, I was traveling at 45 mph. The opposing vehicle starts in traffic to cross the road. I tried to swerve and avoid the collision but was struck hard enough to knock me off course as the opposing vehicle collides into the right side of my car. The seatbelt locked as it was designed and kept me firmly in my seat. Because of that, I was able to brake and steer the vehicle to a stop, avoiding the light pole in my redirected path. Had I not been wearing my seatbelt, the side impact force would have shifted the vehicle out of my control and I would have hit the pole head on. Knowing what I know now about accident investigations and the resultant of forces, I probably would not have survived that impact with the pole if I was not wearing my seatbelt.

Now, as a forensic accident investigator and driving instructor, I get frustrated when someone is killed, ejected from a vehicle or even seriously hurt or disabled because they chose not to wear a seatbelt. It is simple. Get in, sit and buckle up. There are no more excuses, only results.

Airbags

The common term is airbag. It is actually a supplemental restraining system or SRS designed to work in unison with your seatbelt. Remember that your seatbelt is the primary occupant restraint device. Airbags are supplemental to the seatbelts. When both are used properly, your risk of injury is reduced even more than just a seatbelt.

When you are properly belted in the seat, the seatbelt is designed to lock into place upon impact or any great change in momentum or velocity. We have all tugged on the shoulder strap and find that it locks prematurely or when we do not want it to lock. That is because it had some form of rapid change in velocity, especially while the vehicle is in motion. Today's seatbelts are also controlled by a vehicle computer that monitors the vehicle operation in so many areas. Seatbelts are designed to manually lock under certain conditions and also electronically locked under certain condition.

Airbags or SRS are electronically monitored from one of the many vehicle computers called an airbag control module or ACM. Today's newer vehicles have sensors in the seats. Perhaps even in your own vehicle you may have noticed an indicator light that reacts when a front seat passenger is present or not. The front seats have sensors to let the computer know someone is seated there. This is based on a person or object weighing more than 40 pounds. Once the sensor detects that information, it prepares the passenger front seat SRS to activate upon certain types of impacts. If no one is seated and belted, that side may or may not be deployed upon impact, circumstances prevailing.

Not all impacts will cause the SRS to activate and deploy the airbags. Frontal collisions with a determined closing or impact speed will activate the frontal airbags. Some angular collisions may deploy the airbags. Rear end collisions will not activate any airbags unless there are other types of collisions involved such as post impact side collisions or post impact frontal collisions, etc.

Remember this one important fact. As a vehicle collides with an object, let us say for example a front head-on collision, the vehicle begins to crush and crumble from the impact and are designed to for safety reasons as shown in *Figure 10*. As the front of the vehicles crush, there is a rapid change in speed or momentum. The seatbelts have already engaged or locked. Now everything in the car is still moving forward, including you (Inertia). The seatbelt limits the driver and passenger's further movement towards the steering wheel and or dashboard. Just as the belt has locked into place and you are slowing your rate forward due to the belt, the SRS is activated. The impact has already reached its maximum potential when the airbags are deployed. In accident investigation, this is called the maximum engagement of the collision. Remember everything is moving so fast that once the vehicles touch, this is the point of no return. It is happening so fast that only computers can work in milliseconds and activate safety features. The airbags deploy at speeds of over 200 miles per hour. That is half the time it takes too blink your eye. You will not see the airbag(s) deploy. Your sense of awareness will be in such disarray, you will not really remember the actual collision. Only before and after the collision.

Without wearing a seatbelt, your injuries will be greatly increased and the airbags will act as another object in the way of the dashboard and may not be your friend. So please, wear your seatbelt and wear it properly. Wear the shoulder portion in the front of your body and not tucked under your arm as many do. You will only increase your injury potential if it is not worn properly. Do not rely on the use of the SRS devices. Just know they are there to back up the seatbelt system.

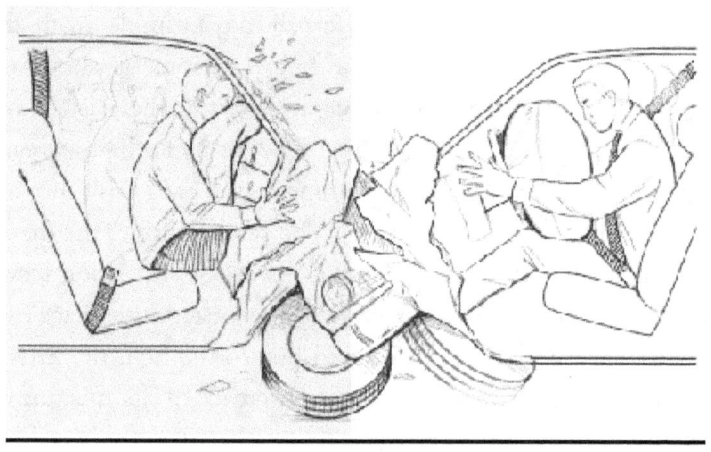

No seatbelt worn   v.   Seatbelt worn

(Figure 10)

Driving Systems

Let us face it; there are many types of driving methods and teachings out there. Two of the most popular are the S.I.P.D.E. method and the Smith-System. Both are very similar and when they are combined, offer an excellent source of driver information to learn, even as a refresher for an experienced driver. These systems are not all encompassing but are a great representation of teaching methods that are available. I learned on the S.I.P.D.E. method. It depends on the preference of the driving instructor and their experience. To understand and utilize both will enhance your driving skills. Let us take a look.

The S.I.P.D.E Method

When reviewing this method, I realized that most of the driving technique is actually the human element. Realistically, the vehicle is a mere extension of the human element, the driver. As we discuss the S.I.P.D.E. method you will realize how much the human element dominates the driver thoughts and actions. The remaining actions are forces applied to and against the vehicle. About 80 percent of the process is visual and mental processing. The remaining 20 percent is the physical application to the driving aspect such as steering, braking and control. The S.I.P.D.E. method will be discussed in detail.

The **S.I.P.D.E.** method is simply;

Search for potential problems.
Identify the problem
Predict what is about to happen
Determine the appropriate actions to avoid collision
Execute that decision.

Searching for constant dangers can be a daunting task. The human eye has evolved as a hunter. It hunts, searches, scans and observes. To utilize this to the maximum potential, the driver must be on constant watch for distant dangers, intermediate possible dangers and close-up dangers. The driver must be aware of what is happening all around them with a 360 degree view. Constantly searching for dangers and more importantly, a way out!

While searching the road ahead for potential danger, you identify a problem. As a practical example, you are driving along a road and a disabled vehicle is a distance ahead. The vehicle is blocking your travel lane on a long straight road with the hazard lights flashing. Currently there are no known on-coming vehicles that you can see. It is that simple. You just identified a problem.

As you approach the identified hazard, the vehicle with the lights flashing, you predict that you will have to approach slowly, signal to change lanes and proceed around the vehicle. In the meantime, you are always searching, identifying and predicting other possible dangers until you pass the vehicle. All of the "What if..." questions now arise. What if an animal darts out in front of you? What if a child or person enters the roadway? What if another vehicle enters the road from an intersecting street or crosses the centerline in your lane? You are constantly in the search and identify mode while driving the vehicle. What if you are in heavy traffic? How does that change your approach?

Thankfully, nothing happened as you approach the disable vehicle. You are ready to decide what actions to take. You could slow down, speed up, maintain current speed or even close your eyes and hope for the best (don't do that). As you approach the vehicle you execute your plan and safely maneuver around the car and continue on your way. You just completed the S.I.P.D.E method of driving and did not even know it. In fact, you do it all the time and may not realize it. It is millisecond, micro processing at its finest, in the blink of an eye or in a heartbeat. It is all human processing and actions that projects into vehicle operations.

The Smith-System Method

Another method is called the SMITH-SYSTEM. The Smith-System was devised back in 1952 from a driving instructor, Harold Smith. "Driving is not about hands and feet it is all about the eyes and mind." The Smith-System is a variant to the S.I.P.D.E method. The Smith-System reports the Smith Five Keys™:

1. **"Aim High in Steering®.** Look further ahead than other drivers." Always look through the cars in front of you and further down the road and plan for a problem to arise.

2.   **"Get the Big Picture®.** Seeing more around you than other drivers." Do not just look in front of you. There are traffic issues to the sides and the rear of your vehicle. Know what is going on around you at all times.

3.   **Keep Your Eyes Moving®.** Being more aware of other drivers."   Keep looking all around your vehicle knowing where vehicle positions are and looking for pedestrians, bicycles, and emergency vehicles.

4.   **"Leave Yourself an Out®.** Positioning in traffic better than other drivers." Drive in a manner that you can escape collision if needed. Leave enough space between vehicles and do not ride in the blind spot of others. Leave yourself an out and do not trust the other actions of other drivers.

5.   **"Make Sure They See You®.**   Make yourself more visible to other drivers." As mentioned above, do not ride in someone's blind spot. Turn on your headlights even in day time.

(source: http://www.smith-system.com/downloads/drive-different.pdf)

So as you can see, there is similarity between the two systems. Each has their own perspective but is virtually the same. Choose which one works best for you. With either system, you cannot go wrong.

Perception and Reaction

Each and every person has what is called a Perception/Reaction time. Perception/Reaction time is simply the time it takes for a driver to perceive a problem and react to the danger. Not every driver perceives and reacts in the same amount of time. Some factors that slow the time period could be age, mental clarity, fatigue, intoxication, distractions, and more. The more combinations present, the greater the Perception/Reaction time.

A modest mean for all around age and daytime perception/reaction time is about 1.5 seconds. That is the time takes from the perception of danger to the reaction of the driver (taking action). At night time, the Perception/Reaction time greatly increases to a modest average up to 3 seconds. This time does not include the response of the vehicle and the time it takes to complete the maneuver such as breaking or evasive steering, only the processing of information, receiving and reacting.

Here is a simple example and some math; speed is derivative of velocity. Velocity is a measurement of distance divided by time or a measurement of how far you have traveled over a period of time and results in feet per second. Speed (miles per hour) is a conversion of velocity (feet per second) divided by 1.466 (a mathematical constant). For example, if you are traveling at 40 feet per second, divided by the mathematical constant of 1.466, then you are traveling 27.28 mph. To convert miles per hour to velocity, simply multiply the miles per hour by 1.466 to obtain the product in feet per seconds.

As a practical example, you are traveling at the posted speed of 25 miles per hour in a neighborhood. At a speed of 25 mph, your velocity is about 36.65 feet per second. By the time you perceive a child running out from between two parked cars and apply emergency braking, you have traveled about 55 feet or two or three car lengths from your front bumper. Then the vehicle has to respond to the braking application. Add another 1.35 seconds and 25 or so feet for braking and you have traveled a total distance of about 80 feet (four to five car lengths) in about 2.8 seconds in time, all in perfect conditions. At night time it is a longer distance due to the Perception / Reaction time difference.

At least for now, you can relate to and understand how the process works. Understanding how it works, you can now correct old habits and create new positive skills. Remember, drivers can always be re-trained and should be from time to time.

I instruct my driving students to always prepare themselves for your next vehicle maneuver. In other words, continue to think ahead. If you are planning to back into a parking space, set yourself up properly before the parking maneuver begins. If you are going to drive into a parking position, prepare yourself before entering the parked position. If you know you want to turn right at the next stop sign, prepare yourself and place your vehicle appropriately at the intersection for a safe and proper turn. By always thinking ahead, you will conduct it subconsciously and reduce driving time and stress.

Driven To Distraction

In today's society, distractions are everywhere. People take driving cars for granted and a regular daily task without really thinking about potential consequences. As humans we are driven to distraction, some more than others. Multitasking is not built into our system. It is a learned behavior.

Studies have been conducted by groups of scientists and revealed that having just one passenger in the car dramatically increases distraction. That number multiplies to great numbers for each person added in the vehicle. Any task other than driving the vehicle is distracting and removes the focus on driving.

Cell phones come to mind. There are great arguments going back and forth about the use of hands free devices to keep hands on the wheel. Realistically, hands-free devices only allow the driver to use free hands for some other form of distraction such as stereo manipulation, eating, drinking, or something else. The argument behind talking on the cell phone while driving or even worse, texting while driving, is that the driver's attention is focused somewhere else besides focusing on the task of driving. Conversations distract and delay response time while driving a vehicle. The same as chemical impairment like alcohol or drugs. Texting while driving is the same as closing your eyes while driving. Sound like a good idea? Not if you want to stay alive or not crash. Who in their right mind would close their eyes for three to five seconds while driving at interstate speed 65-80 miles per hour or any speed for that matter? Those that text and drive, that's who! Pay attention to your driving or pay someone else, if you survive.

CHAPTER 4

CONNECTING VEHICLE AND DRIVER

ANDRE R. LEVESQUE

Vehicle Selection

As newer vehicles are designed and manufactured, many of the newer vehicles are equipped with adjustable features that accommodate drivers in one way or another. Now, with the standardization of passenger compartment side airbags, sitting too close to the steering wheel is dangerous and may create unnecessary injury to the driver. For example, the invention of a tilt steering wheel, and recently telescoping and tilting steering wheel, have assisted drivers of all physiques allowing the driver to seat themselves at a safer distance from the wheel in the event of an air bag deployment.

Another feature is motorized adjustments of the pedals, allowing the pedals to move closer to the seated driver and allow the driver to remain a safe distance from the wheel. This is a great assistance to those that are of shorter stature or have particular disabilities. It is primarily a comfort issue but can be thought of as a positive safety feature as well. If you are unsure the vehicle you are driving has these features, read your owner's manual, ask the manufacturer or check with a local dealer or mechanic.

Everyone has a preference for vehicles. Some like brand new ones some prefer used, some like antiques or classics. In any case, how many times have we witnessed drivers operating vehicles that they just do not seem to fit the vehicle? The driver that is barely tall enough to see over the dashboard and you can only see fingers on the top of the wheel? What about the person that looks like a woolly mammoth in a cigar box? We have all seen these people and wonder how they can drive the car safely. It is important to find a vehicle that fits you, the driver. It is recommend that the person who drives the vehicle should have the most say in driver area features and safety. Passenger comfort comes secondary. It is important to consider vehicle size, driver seating placement and visibility. Here are some things to consider when selecting a vehicle to drive:

• Can you adjust the steering wheel so that your chest is at least 12 to 14 inches away from the wheel?

• In a proper seated position, you should be able to reach the steering wheel, place your wrists at the top of the wheel leaving your hands to fall over the top.

• While in this seated position, can you safely reach the floor pedals with your feet and apply them to the maximum position without moving your body?

• Can you reach the controls on the dashboard with limited movement forward from the proper seated position?

• Can you view 360 degrees around the vehicle by looking forward and utilizing all provided rearview mirrors?

Motor vehicle manufacturers have been developing adjustable features to safely accommodate drivers of all statures. Some of these features are telescoping steering columns and telescoping foot pedals, power seats and power mirrors. When speaking to a sales person or driving instructor, ask about these features to seat yourself properly and safely. (Remember that sales staff may not be properly trained in this area and may just be concerned about the sale.)

Proper Seating Position

Proper seating position is essential to the safe operation of the vehicle. Why? I am glad you asked. It allows the driver to have better control of the vehicle and may reduce injury in the event of a collision. Each person has a preferred seating position; some due to physical size or limitation, others by comfort. Neither is necessarily wrong, so long as you can safely operate the vehicle with two hands on the wheel and can see 360 degrees around you. A recommended seating position is either straight up or one or two levels away from the straight up position. The further back you recline, your visibility is lessened and the more likely you are to be distracted.

We have all seen the drivers that are almost lying down and or leaning on the center arm rest with their left hand on the top of the wheel. Although it may be the driver's preferred method, it is not the safest method for vehicle operation. These drivers are usually more concerned with other matters like their music, comfort and other mental distractions rather than operating a vehicle safely.

Steering Wheel - Hand Position and Steering Methods

Most to all driving instructors will utilize the two handed steering wheel grip. Arguments go back and forth regarding the effectiveness of the two handed versus the one handed. It has been shown that proper two handed wheel control is safer and allows the driver more control of the vehicle in normal and emergency control situations. In a very marginal range of situations, one handed operations can be safely utilized with advanced training.

By not safely controlling the vehicle with two handed wheel operation, it is easy for the driver to under-steer and over-steer the vehicle or simply lose control in certain driving situations. With proper training, two handed wheel operation becomes natural and will automatically engage in emergent situations since the hands are already on the wheel. More steering operations are discussed further in Chapter 5.

So what is the proper hand placement on the wheel? Hand placement mirrors the hands on a clock (*Figure 11*). The old "Ten and Two" application was standard and may still be taught today (Left hand in the ten o'clock position and the right hand in the two o'clock position). By utilizing this technique, it may cause driver fatigue, vehicle sway with a lack of concentration and is more prone to cause over-steering or under-steering situations.

A better hand placement on the wheel is the "Nine and Three" method (left hand in the nine o'clock position and the right hand in the three o'clock position). Race car drivers and drivers that operate at high speeds discovered that this method works better to prevent under-steering and over-steering issues. By placing the hands in this position allows the driver to safely maintain control of the vehicle and reduces driver fatigue. More importantly, it keeps the hands and arms out of the way of air bag deployment in the event of a frontal collision (*Figure 12*).

If hands are placed in the "Ten and Two" position, the deployment of the airbag will push against the forearms causing the arms to be forced back toward the driver at 200+ mph (the force and speed of airbag deployments). This causes unnecessary injury to the driver's arms and head. Driving instructors should properly demonstrate the difference in vehicle control with the two hand positions to allow you to see the difference.

The "Nine and Three" method also allows the driver more steering stability if one hand is removed from the wheel. This allows the driver to turn the wheel 180 degrees in either direction with either hand. After proper demonstration from your instructor, you will discover that you can drive with one hand but only in those obscure situations where the second hand is unavailable. In other words, if you happen to be reaching for that drink in the cup holder and an emergency lane change is in order to avoid collision, you will be able to handle the emergency maneuver. Other than that, leave your hands on the wheel. Palming the wheel or with one hand at the top, with two fingers is just not safe for any type of driving especially in the event of an emergency.

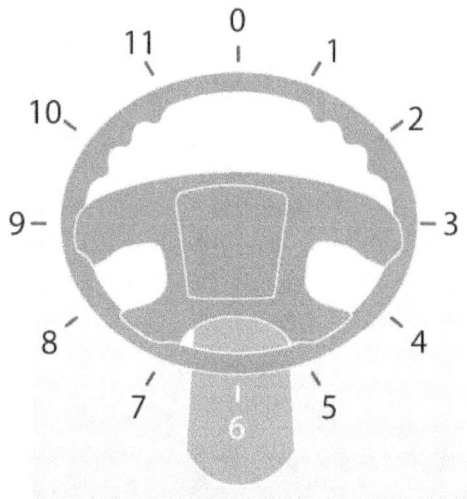

(Figure 11)

(Figure 12)

Turning Cues and Pivot Points

We all see different types of vehicles on the road. Whether it is small or large, the basic vehicle characteristics are the same. All cars or automobiles have similar features on the vehicle such as wheel placement, axles that hold the wheels, steering, passenger compartment or cage design and turning or pivot points. Again, all vehicles makes and models are different but all operate on the same principals.

For example, you have entered a parking space at the store. The parking space is straight and you are parked perfectly in that space. Now that shopping is done, you want to leave. Before you back out, you check your mirrors, look over your shoulder and verify the space is clear, right? Well you should anyway. Now you may begin to back. The question is now apparent. When do I turn my wheels to safely maneuver around the vehicles next to me? Similarly, you are entering a parked position you ask the same question. This is where you should know the size limitations of your vehicle well ahead of time and understand the turning or pivot points of the vehicle.

Whether backing or even driving forward, knowing where your turning pivot points are located on the vehicle is very important. It will save you many trips to the body shop. When backing the vehicle, the pivot point is very different. Then driving forward. As you back the vehicle, the pivot point is the rear axle or rear wheel. When the rear axle or tire reaches the area that is open to turn (the rear of the adjacent vehicle), that is the point where you need to begin turning the front wheels to maneuver the vehicle safely.

All vehicles are required to have windshields. The steel framework on the side of the vehicles that hold the windshield in place and connects to the roof is called the "A" pillar. In a four door sedan model car or just behind the driver seat area is a secondary pillar where the door(s) come to a close and the seatbelts are generally attach is called the "B" pillar. The rear window frame work at the rear of the vehicle is called a "C" pillar.

There are two turning or pivot points to consider, the front wheels (front axle) and the rear wheels (rear axle) as depicted in *Figure 13* below.

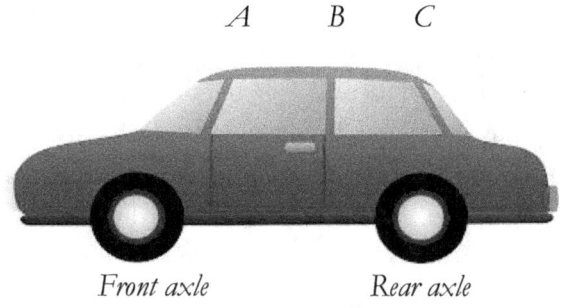

(Figure 13)

When the vehicle is moving forward and you wish to turn the vehicle into a parking space or a similar 90 degree turn, the general area pivot point should be just before or at the "B' pillar. Most vehicles fall between the "A" and "B" pillar. To make sure the rear of the vehicle does not collide with the other parked car, The "B" pillar is best used.

It may seem wasteful, but try making 90 degree turns at each and every intersection movement you conduct. When at a stop sign and want to turn right, do not cheat to the right then stop. It creates bad habits and will be sure to get you a ticket for running the stop sign at some point. Approach the stop sign with your intended signal and stop at the stop bar like you were intending to travel straight. When the right of way has been yielded to you, proceed to make the turn at a 90 degree angle. You can ensure a few events will occur; you will not be likely to run the stop sign, you will be less likely to strike the curb and most importantly you will be able to see the entire intersection, other vehicles, pedestrians and bicycles to!

Here is a tip to consider when you want to turn a vehicle immediately from a cold stop such as parallel parking or tight spaces. Before the vehicle is set in motion, turn the steering wheel in the appropriate direction before the vehicle is set in motion. This allows the vehicle to respond faster and will prevent unnecessary back and forth movements to align the vehicle properly. If you begin turning the wheels after the vehicle is in motion, you may lose or waste precious space to maneuver the vehicle. If the wheels are already turned prior to movement, the vehicle is ready to head in that direction before the vehicle moves. Always think ahead to your next maneuver when driving a car and set yourself up for the next turn or movement.

Using Mirrors

Mirrors are required on vehicles to assist the driver in viewing areas behind the driver. Regular automobiles are designed with three mirrors installed on the vehicle. One on the driver door, one on the passenger door and one inside the passenger compartment as a center mirror.

The driver should have the center mirror positioned to see the entire rear window of the vehicle and maximize the view to the rear of the vehicle. The driver side mirror should be positioned even with the road surface and positioned so the driver may view to the rear. The right outside mirror should be positioned in a similar fashion but to view the right side of the vehicle. See *Figure 14* for suggested positioning views.

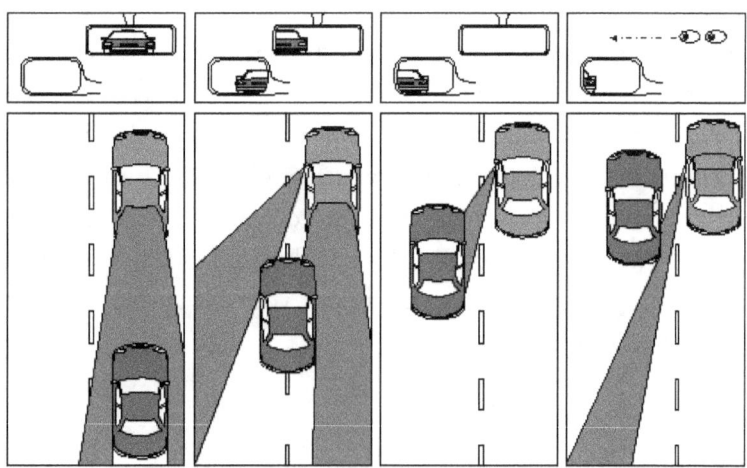

Figure 14

A dynamic driver should be able to sit and face forward in the vehicle viewing 180 degrees forward. Also, the dynamic driver should be able to sit, face forward and view 180 degrees to the rear by using the mirrors. This provides 360 degrees of viewing with little movement by the driver and little view from the roadway ahead.

Using mirrors properly and on a regular basis takes practice and is an intentional effort. Start by using the mirrors in a conscious effort all the time. Eventually it will become second nature. This also helps those with physical disabilities that may prohibit some movement of the driver. Give it an honest try. You may like it (I hope you do).

Using the mirrors properly when backing is also essential. It will not eliminate all blind spots but it is easier. It also reduces blind spots that occur when looking over your shoulder. Remember to constantly check all mirrors when backing and constantly be aware of your surroundings. Anything can happen at any time and it will when backing since it is not a normal direction of travel.

Vehicles that are equipped with rear view cameras that activate when backing can assist the driver. However, I do not recommend it as the only view you should have when backing. When you get used to backing with mirrors and can successfully do so, the video monitor can then be used as an additional mirror for close proximity backing or use the audible alerts only for backing. To rely solely on the camera sets you up for failure as a driver especially when technology fails.

ANDRE R. LEVESQUE

CHAPTER 5

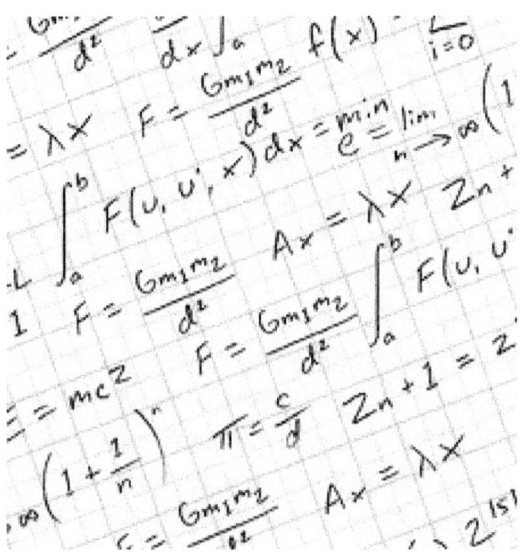

UNDERSTANDING VEHICLE DYNAMICS

(More science stuff)

ANDRE R. LEVESQUE

Understanding Vehicle Dynamics

Vehicle dynamics refers to the dynamic movement of vehicles, here assumed to be ground vehicles. Vehicle dynamics is a part of engineering primarily based on classical mechanics. As mentioned above, all vehicles operate within Newton's Laws of Physics. A motor vehicle will travel in whatever direction and rate of speed that is controlled by the driver. A vehicle generally does not want to drive in a straight direction and generally does not want to stop due to the motor in operation and the vehicle transmission. So it is up to the driver to control the vehicle. There are a few more basic physics principals that a driver needs to fully understand; motion and weigh transfer.

Center of Mass / Center of Gravity

One way to define the center of gravity of a vehicle is simply a total balancing point. Consider a vehicle like a flat board resting on the tip of an upside down top. The very center of a uniform sized board will be the center of gravity or center of mass. Imagine finding the balancing point of a lopsided log. It will be more difficult to find and may not be in the center of the log as it was on the board. In other words, every object has a balancing point, a center of mass or a center of gravity. This center of gravity is an invisible location and exists only when the force is uniform, in which case it coincides with the center of mass. This approach dates back to Archimedes from ancient Greece.

Every object, no matter how large or small, has a center of gravity (COG) or center of mass (COM). People and vehicles have a center of mass. In a general view, for people the center of mass is located in the waist area. As for vehicles, it is located just behind the windshield area or dashboard area (each vehicle has a unique or different center of mass location and this example is generic in nature). The center of mass is used to calculate lateral, directional and rotational motion. To understand the center of mass concept will greatly improve your understanding the vehicle handling. Consider the center of mass a pivot point of motion and how the vehicle maneuvers.

Vehicle Acceleration

When a vehicle accelerates, weight transfers toward the rear wheels. An outside observer might witness this as the vehicle visibly leans to the back, or squats. Conversely, while braking, weight transfer toward the front of the car will occur. Under hard braking, it might be clearly visible even from inside the vehicle as the nose dives toward the ground (most of this will be due to load transfer). Similarly, during changes in direction (lateral or circular motion), weight transfer to the outside of the turn will occur as part of centripital force.

In an academic perspective, when the driver presses on the accelerator the force created by the vehicle drive axle and wheels forces the vehicle forward. Realistically we feel that we are being pushed backwards. We have all experienced that. This is Newton's Laws at work. The vehicle acts on one principal and the occupants and contents in the vehicle act under a different principal.

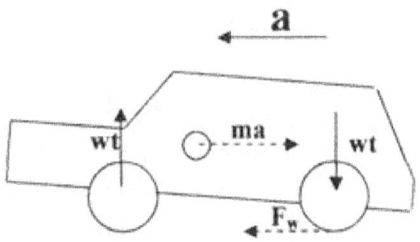

Car under acceleration

(Figure 15)

The area labeled as "ma" in the above illustration indicates the invisible center of mass for the vehicle. As the center of mass is accelerated forward, weight is transferred to the rear of the vehicle. The faster the acceleration, the faster the weight is transferred to the rear and more weight is transferred to the rear of the vehicle. This is important to understand all vehicles both front wheel drive and rear wheel drive vehicles *(Figure 14)*.

For rear wheel drive vehicles, as a vehicle accelerates, more weight is transferred to the rear drive axle, therefore providing more weight and force to the rear drive axle. However in front-wheel drive vehicles, severe or rapid acceleration reduces weight to the front vehicle drive axle and reduces the front axle friction with the roadway. Ultimately it reduces tire traction and steering potential when rapid acceleration is present.

Vehicle Negative Acceleration

When a vehicle slows, the opposite takes place. All the same principals of physics apply, only in a negative format. Just as when the vehicle weight shifts in an acceleration period, weight transferred in a negative acceleration period (In the scientific world, the term, "deceleration", actually does not exist. It is referred to as a negative acceleration). The harder the brakes are applied to slow the vehicle, the faster the weight is transferred forward (Figure 16). This force is understood as the vehicle front end dips towards the roadway and we are forced against our seatbelts until the force becomes equal or the vehicle stops.

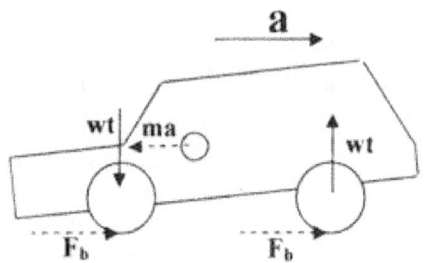

Car under deceleration

(Figure 16)

As the vehicle slows weight is transferred to the front of the vehicle and onto the front axle or the steering axle of the vehicle. This force actually works in our favor allowing more friction between the front tires and the surface of the roadway. This increase in friction provides more steering grip, which in turn allows for better steering response if needed. It also reduces the weight on the rear axle and creates less traction to the rear tires, which in turn may work against us due to poor traction in the rear.

The full understanding of these principals is essential in driving dynamics as they are actually applied in advanced Behind-the-Wheel type of driver training.

Vehicle Steering and Cornering

Since we have learned how the vehicle moves during acceleration and negative acceleration, let us throw in a few more factors to understand. Friction is just as important to understand as any other principal. Friction is a physical force resisting the kinetic motion of solid surfaces as they move across one another. For example, if you rub your hands together fast and hard, it creates heat. This heat is actually a thermal transfer of energy from the kinetic motion and contact between the two surfaces of your hands. The faster and harder you rub, the faster heat is generated. Dry friction resists relative lateral motion of two solid surfaces in contact. The two regimes of dry friction are static friction between non-moving surfaces, and kinetic friction (sometimes called sliding friction or dynamic friction) between moving surfaces.

Understanding friction and weight transfer is imperative in vehicle operations; especially cornering. We understand that when accelerating, weight is transferred to the rear drive axle, thus allowing force to be applied against the road surface. Friction between the tire and the road surface allows the vehicle tire to "grip" the road surface. When the friction force is not equal between the roadway surface and tire surface, it causes the tire to loose grip with the road and can either cause the vehicle to slide or loose lateral friction. This can cause the driver to lose control of the vehicle.

Vehicle body roll is a reference to the load transfer of a vehicle towards the outside of a turn. When a vehicle is fitted with a suspension package, it works to keep the wheels in contact with the road, providing stability for the driver allowing better control. This suspension is compliant to some degree, allowing the vehicle body, which sits upon the suspension, to lean in the direction of the perceived centripetal force acting upon the car. Anti-roll bars are a part of the suspension specifically designed to address and resist body roll.

When a vehicle is fitted with a suspension there is compliance between the mass of the vehicle and the vehicle's contact with the ground. Body roll is the noticeable (either perceived or measurable) deflection produced when load transfer acts on the compliant elements of the suspension. Anti-roll bars directly impact body roll but their design intent is actually as a tool to adjust roll couple percentage or roll moment distribution. In simple terms, it limits the top of the vehicle from swaying back and forth. The stiffer the suspension the less the vehicle will sway.

Steering Input and Control

Under-steer and over-steer are vehicle dynamic terms used to describe the sensitivity of a vehicle to steering. In general, steering input is how much you actually turn the steering wheel. Automotive engineers define under-steer and over-steer based on changes in steering angle associated with changes in lateral acceleration over a sequence of steady-state circular turning tests. Car and motorsport enthusiasts often use the terminology more generally in magazines and blogs to describe vehicle response to steering in all kinds of maneuvers.

When an under-steer vehicle is taken to frictional limits where it is no longer possible to increase lateral acceleration, the vehicle will follow a path with a radius larger than intended. Although the vehicle cannot increase lateral acceleration, it is dynamically stable. This means that when you understeer you will not make the curve or turn (*Figure 17*).

When an over-steer vehicle is taken to frictional limits, it becomes dynamically unstable with a tendency to spin out. Although the vehicle is unstable in open-loop control, a skilled driver can maintain control a little past the point of instability with counter-steering (sometimes called drifting). However, at some limit in lateral acceleration, it is not physically possible for even the most skilled driver to maintain a steady state and spinout will occur (*Figure 17*).

Simply put, over-steer is what occurs when a car turns (steers) by more than (over) the amount commanded by the driver. Conversely, under-steer is what occurs when a car steers less than (under) the amount commanded by the driver.

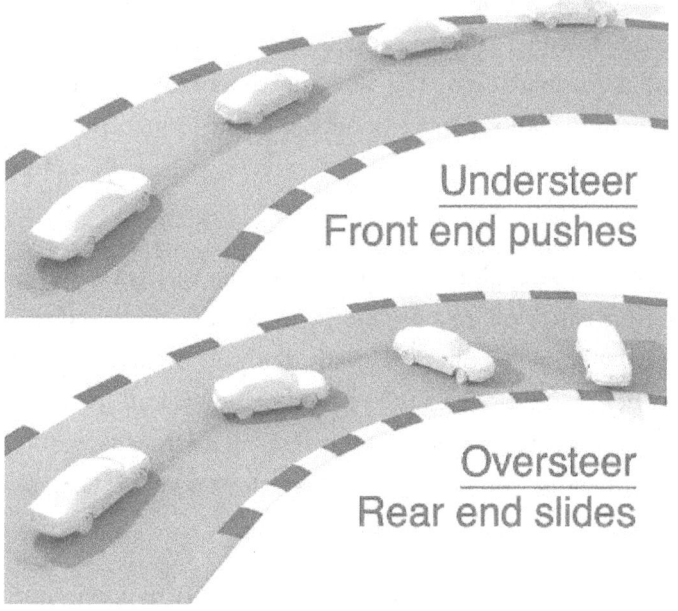

(Figure 17)

Traveling in Circles

Thrill rides. Most of us like them some thrive for them. One thing for sure, we have all experienced some of the same forces in one form or another in vehicles. There is a force that pushes you outward when traveling in circles at high speeds. That feeling that you want to fly out of the car or ride but the door or ride safety harness keeps you in your seat. This force is called centripetal force. Centripetal force is defined as "the force that is necessary to keep an object moving in a curved path and that is directed inward toward the center of rotation" (Mririam-Webster, 2014).

As a car makes a turn, the force of friction acting upon the turned wheels of the car provides centripetal force required for circular motion. When centripetal force meets or exceeds the resistant (net) force, the object, in this case the vehicle will break loose. The unbalanced force and the acceleration are both directed towards the center of the circle about which the car is turning. While the car is accelerating inward, you continue in a straight line outward.

If you are sitting on the passenger side of the car, then eventually the outside door of the car will hit you as the car turns inward. This is the sensation of an outward force and an outward acceleration thus creating a false sensation. There is no physical object capable of pushing you outwards. You merely experience the tendency of your body continuing its path tangent to the circular path along which the car is turning. Centripetal force is also the second aspect of Newton's law of inertia - "an object in motion tends to stay in motion with the same speed and in the same direction... ."

Traction / Friction

Load (weight) transfer causes the available traction at all four wheels to vary as the car brakes, accelerates, or turns. This bias to one pair of tires doing more "work" than the other pair results in a net loss of total available traction. The net loss can be attributed to the phenomenon known as tire load sensitivity.

An exception is during positive acceleration when the engine power is driving two or fewer wheels. In this situation where all the tires are not being utilized load transfer can be advantageous. As such, the most powerful cars are almost never front wheel drive, as the acceleration itself causes the front wheels' traction to decrease. This is why sports cars usually have either rear wheel drive or all-wheel drive (and in the all-wheel drive case, the power tends to be biased toward the rear wheels under normal conditions).

Speed

Nobody speeds, right? Well if you believe that I have a unicorn for sale. At some point, whether intended or not, we all exceed the speed limit. People generally are within 5 miles per hour over the posted speed limit and find that acceptable. I am no hypocrite. I have done my share of exceeding the posted speed limit. Whether it is 1 mph over or 30 mph over, speeding is speeding. What is most important is how speed affects the dynamics of driving. Faster speed means faster mental processing, faster reactions, longer braking distance and possibly a loss of control.

As previously mentioned, speed is a conversion of velocity. Velocity is measured in feet per second whereas speed is measured in miles per hour. Velocity is a measurement of distance traveled in a determined amount of time. Speed is such an important factor to understand. If you are traveling at a safe speed than you should be able to correctly handle most incidents or emergencies in your path, right? Just because a road is posted 45 miles per hour (mph) does not mean that you have to drive at 45 mph despite what the other drivers feel. The white posted 45 mph sign, or whatever the posted speed sign displays, is a maximum allowed speed. That is an absolute speed in most states. That means that 46 or more is in violation regardless if you are traveling or passing. The yellowish orange signs posted at curves or off ramps are posted warning speeds as a warning that higher speeds may not be favorable in this roadway design or conditions.

For example, a sharp curve may have a curve warning sign with a suggested lower speed to safely maneuver the curve. The choice is yours to exceed the posted speed limit or adhere to the posted maximum speed. However, a dynamic driver already has enough mental processing in the works; they do not need to calculate more with speed conversions. Does five miles per hour really make a difference?

Here is another practical example. The road you are traveling is posted at 45 miles per hour. Remember that miles per hour is velocity and with the proper conversion, the velocity is measured at 66 (65.97 actual) feet per second. During the day your perception and reaction time is about 1.5 seconds from the perception of the problem to your initial reaction to the emergency. By multiplying the velocity of 66 fps by the time of 1.5 seconds, you have now traveled almost 99 feet before the vehicle is reacting to your decision.

At 40 mph you are traveling at a velocity of about 59 (58.64 actual) feet per second with a 1.5 second perception and reaction time. At 40 mph you will travel 88 (87.96) feet. The difference of the 5 mph is about 11 feet; a little less than one car length. In a panic or emergency straight braking scenario, that 5 mph can make the difference between a rear end collision and avoiding the collision. At night time that five miles per hour difference with a perception / reaction time of 3.5 seconds changes the distance to 231 feet at 45 mph to 205 feet at 40 mph. At night time, the speed variation of 5 mph doubles the distance. Because it takes longer to perceive and react at night, that one car length increases to two or three car lengths. In the same scenario, in the daytime you may avoid the rear end collision but at night time you will not.

So, does five miles per hour really make a difference?

CHAPTER 6

OTHER INFORMATION, TECHNOLOGY AND TIPS.

ANDRE R. LEVESQUE

When Technology Fails

What happens when technology fails? What do you know about basic driving skills that will make the difference between a collision and avoiding a collision? I ask this because it seems today's vehicles have been designed for marketing purposes. Some purposes have been regulated for safety, but the remainder is consumer driven. It started years ago with the desire for automatic transmissions, power steering, power brakes, power windows, air conditioning.

In the past 25 years, automobile companies have developed anti-lock braking systems to assist drivers and preventing wheel lockup when braking. They have added small things like tire pressure sensors and computer systems to regulate the machine. Recently passed into law, and expected for the 2016 models, mandates auto manufacturers to have some sort of backup displays and camera(s) to prevent a rear end collision when backing. This list can go on and on. But what happens when technology fails?

If you train yourself on the new luxuries of the automobile features and do not master the basics of driving the vehicle and understanding how the various systems in the car work, you can set yourself up for failure. For example, if you break hard and the antilock braking system or ABS does not activate and the car begins to skid, what do you do? Can you avoid a collision with alternative driving and braking techniques? Unless you have a physical disability, does using the rearview mirror make you a superior driver in reverse? What happens if that fails? What happens if the power steering fails? What do you do? How about tire failure on the highway? Do not rely just on these special features that "make a vehicle safe." It is you the driver, which makes the vehicle safe. It is you, the driver, which is responsible for the vehicle's actions while in the driver seat. It is you, the human, and not the machine.

Vehicle Maintenance Tips

Read the Vehicle Owner's Manual

Take the time to read the owner's manual of your vehicle. There is so much important information about driving your vehicle and how to conduct basic maintenance for the vehicle. Each vehicle is different and may have different characteristics that are required to know to safely operate the vehicle. If you have a vehicle that does not have one, they are available on line through the manufacturer website or contact the manufacturer.

Vehicle Features

Learn all the features in your vehicle before driving the vehicle. At the very least learn the basic vehicle operation features; pedals, seat placement, gear shifter, directional, headlamp switch, wiper switch and so one before learning the stereo features and driving off. The stereo should be the last thing you try to figure out. Do not try to learn vehicle features while driving the vehicle. For a refresher, see Driven to Distraction section.

Tires and Tire Pressure

Take the time to understand tire pressure and what the proper pressure for your tires may be. If you have aftermarket tires, be sure to ask the installation professional about minimum and maximum pressures. Minimum pressure has been tested and is measured when the vehicle has not been driven for a while or considered cold. When you measure the pressure in the morning or the vehicle has been parked for a while, an accurate measurement will occur. As the tire is turned and used on the roadway, friction occurs. Friction between the tire and the road surface causes heat. Heat transfers from the tire into the air inside the tire causing it to inflate naturally. You do not want to exceed the maximum pressure or a blowout can occur. Talk to your tire professionals for advice. Do not exceed any tire manufacturer recommendations and alter the tires or wheels. Most vehicles have a tire pressure decal in the door jam on the driver side door. Inspect the area. If it is not there, check with your tire professionals. Tire pressure also impacts and affects your miles per gallon use. If the tire pressure is low, the vehicle must work harder to rotate the tires and in turn uses more fuel.

Vision Obstructions

Many collisions occur due to vision obstructions. These come in different ways. Many are from items hanging from the rear view mirror, glare, not wearing appropriate sun glasses during day time hours, failure to keep the interior and exterior glass clean and streak free and keeping glass decals out of the way of critical and non-critical vision areas. Where allowed, sun shading or window tinting should not exceed the requirements allowed by law. It distorts the view of the driver and severely restricts visibility at night while looking through the side and rear windows. Also keep your passengers in check and limit the motion of the passengers inside the vehicle.

Check under the Hood

Be familiar with the engine compartment. You do not have to be a mechanic to understand how to check fluid levels and other engine compartment features. First know how to open the hood with the latch release feature in the car. Your owner's manual will assist you with this task.

Second, most auto manufacturers have made checking limited items under the hood easy and color coded. Your owner's manual, auto sales person or mechanic can assist you with this. Most are bright colors, like yellow, that are painted on the handles of the areas you should check. If it is not color coded, leave it to the professionals. For example, windshield washer fluid reservoir is usually marked, coolant fluid reservoir, the oil dipstick, the transmission dipstick, where to add oil, etc. Take the time to learn these areas and how to check fluid levels.

Remember, YOU the driver, are responsible for the safe operation of the vehicle. YOU, the owner of the vehicle, are responsible for the vehicle safety and maintenance. Take responsibility for your actions and take responsibility for the vehicle you drive and or own. Your life and or the life of someone else will depend on it.

Headlamps, Tail Lamps, Break Lamps and More

Be sure that all head lamps, tail lamps, break lamps, side marker lights, rear license plate lights are all working and clean from dirt and debris. Clean and clear head lamps improve visibility. Working tail and break lamps, prevent rear end crashes, working turn signals improve driver safety and a better flow of traffic. The last I knew, all vehicle models are equipped with turn signals. Use them!

If you haul a trailer with your vehicle, be sure that a proper wire harness is compatible with the trailer and vehicle, be sure that the ball and hitch are correctly sized and properly secured with safety chains, and be sure that all lights are properly working BEFORE you hit the road.

Driver License and Vehicle Paperwork

States require that when driving a motor vehicle on any roadway, the driver must carry with them, the state issued driver's license card. Even if it is a quick trip to the store, bring it with you.

Be sure that the proper vehicle paperwork is in the vehicle when it is on the roadway. Required by all states, the vehicle registration and proof of insurance documents must be presented to law enforcement officers upon request of the officer in one form or another. Check with your state requirements, as some states allow electronic versions such as cell phone applications as proof of insurance and registration. Each state is different, be sure to check with laws in your state or ask your local law enforcement officials.

If you are hauling a trailer owned by yourself, whether borrowed from a friend or hauling one for your employment, it is you the driver that is responsible to hold the registration of the trailer and have it with you while the trailer is attached. Save yourself some time and aggravation and be sure to have all proper documents when traveling, especially on those short trips.

Let us understand that these are not all encompassing tips but only a mere few to get you thinking. Most importantly, be sure that your vehicle is in good operating condition including tires, brakes, steering, and fluid levels to name a few.

CHAPTER 7

SUMMARY

ANDRE R. LEVESQUE

Now that we understand the physics behind the vehicle and a bit about the driver, let us try to piece it all together. There is more to driving a vehicle than just sitting in the driver seat, starting the vehicle, putting the vehicle in gear and go. We now know that there is more to just driving down the road to get where we want to go. We know that there are physical forces that limit the vehicle and natural processes that limit the driver. The more you practice these simple principles the better you will become. Better yet, realizing and practicing these thoughts each and every time you sit behind the wheel and you will become a safe dynamic driver!

Remember that when you are driving, you are an extension of the vehicle and more so, the vehicle is an extension of you! The vehicle is a machine, a tool, a device used to travel, a tool that can be overwhelming if not understood and used properly. A tool that is deadly in the wrong hands or in control of a distracted, impaired or even an attentive driver. As a dynamic driver, you must always be alert to your surroundings and anticipating problems that do not exist at the moment.

The dynamic driver is a driver that will control the vehicle's actions as it is the driver themselves. The dynamic driver is always observing their surroundings and anticipating the 'what if' scenarios. The dynamic driver limits distractions and impairment from fatigue or intoxication. The dynamic driver is an advanced driver in the area of attentiveness, assertiveness, knowledge of the vehicle, driver ability all while utilizing the vehicle as an extension of the driver. Action is always faster than reaction. If you, the driver, are fatigued or impaired, your reaction time is greatly diminished and more likely to be involved in a collision. No matter what vehicle type you are driving, most concepts are the same. You have one duty as a driver, to drive the vehicle safely. Drive with due regard to other drivers, to the rules of the road and for the safety of yourself, your passengers and the other motoring public.

Drive safe, drive smart!

To Be Continued...........

Bibliography

Merrian-Webster. (2014). *Centripetal Force*. Retrieved 06 08, 2014, from Merriam-Webster.com: http://www.merriam-webster.com/dictionary/centripetal force

Mririam-Webster. (2014). *Cognitive*. Retrieved 05 04, 2014, from Dictionary: http://www.merriam-webster.com/dictionary/cognitive

NASA, National Aeronautics and Space Administration. (2014, June 12). *Newton's First Law*. (T. Benson, Editor) Retrieved July 17, 2014, from NASA Glenn Research Center: http://www.grc.nasa.gov/WWW/k-12/airplane/newton1g.html

NASA, National Aeronautics and Space Administration. (2014, June 12). *Newton's Second Law of Motion*. (T. Benson, Editor) Retrieved July 21, 2014, from NASA Glenn Research Center: http://www.grc.nasa.gov/WWW/k-12/airplane/newton.html

NASA, National Aeronautics and Space Administration. (2014, June 2014). *Newton's Third Law*. (T. Benson, Editor) Retrieved July 2014, 2014, from NASA Glenn Research Center: http://www.grc.nasa.gov/WWW/k-12/airplane/newton.html

Physics4Kids.com. (2014). *Newton's Laws of Physics*. Retrieved July 21, 2014, from Physics4Kids.com: http://www.physics4kids.com/files/motion_laws.html

The Smith System. (2014). *Smith-System*. Retrieved 08 04, 2014, from Smith-System: http://www.smith-system.com/downloads/Drive_Different.pdf

TutorVista. (2014). *Newton's First Law of Motion*. Retrieved July 21, 2014,from utorVista.com: http://physics.tutorvista.com/motion/newton-s-first-law-of-motion.html

ANDRE R. LEVESQUE

ABOUT THE AUTHOR

Mr. Andre "Andy" Levesque has an extensive background in law enforcement, driver training, traffic crash investigation and reconstruction. Mr. Levesque was a law enforcement officer in the State of Maine and later moved his career to the State of Florida to complete his 23 year career. He has been valued as a trainer for law enforcement field operations, high liability instruction for emergency vehicle operations and utilized in his expertise as a traffic enforcement officer, impaired driver investigator, crash investigator and forensic crash reconstruction specialist.

Mr. Levesque currently resides in the Tampa Bay, Florida area and has established his own forensic crash reconstruction and consulting business in addition to driver training and education.